Grouping Words

Sentences

Anita Ganeri

Heinemann Library
Chicago, Illinois

www.capstonepub.com
Visit our website to find out
more information about
Heinemann-Raintree books.

To order:
☎ Phone 888-454-2279
💻 Visit www.capstonepub.com
to browse our catalog and order online.

© 2012 Heinemann Library
an imprint of Capstone Global Library, LLC
Chicago, Illinois

Edited by Daniel Nunn, Rebecca Rissman, and Sian Smith
Designed by Joanna Hinton-Malivoire
Picture research by Tracy Cummins
Original illustrations © Capstone Global Library
Illustrated by Joanna Hinton-Malivoire
Production by Eirian Griffiths
Originated by Capstone Global Library Ltd
Printed and bound in China by South China Printing
Company Ltd

15 14 13 12 11
10 9 8 7 6 5 4 3 2 1

Library of Congress Cataloging-in-Publication Data
Ganeri, Anita, 1961-
  Grouping words : sentences / Anita Ganeri.
    p. cm.—(Getting to grips with grammar)
  Includes bibliographical references and index.
ISBN 978-1-4329-5809-1 (hbk) ISBN 978-1-4329-5816-9 (pbk)
1. English language—Sentences—Juvenile literature. 2. English
language—Grammar—Juvenile literature. I. Title.
  PE1441.G36 2011
    428.2—dc22   2011014970

Acknowledgments
We would like to thank the following for permission to reproduce
photographs and artworks: istockphoto pp.22 (© Mark Murphy),
23 (© Ben Blankenburg), 27 (© Elena Elisseeva); Shutterstock
pp.5 (© Vishnevskiy Vasily), 6 (© Chris Howey), 7 (© Danilo
Sanino), 8 (© Eric Isselée), 9 (© Cheryl E. Davis), 10 (© Gorban),
11 (© Alena Ozerova), 12 (© Monkey Business Images), 13 (©
Jorg Hackemann), 14 (© NIKSPHOTO dot COM), 15 (© Julien
Tromeur), 16 (© Granite), 17 (© Monkey Business Images), 18 (©
Cheryl Casey), 19 (© Roger De Marfa), 20 (© maribell), 21 (© Elisei
Shafer), 24 (© Alexia Khruscheva), 25 (© David Grigg), 26 (©
Belinka), 28 (© Zoran Vukmanov Simokov), 30 (© David Ma¡ka).

Every effort has been made to contact copyright holders of any
material reproduced in this book. Any omissions will
be rectified in subsequent printings if notice is given to
the publisher.

Contents

Some words are shown in bold, **like this**.
You can find them in the glossary on page 31.

What Is Grammar?

Grammar is a set of rules that helps you to write and speak a language. Grammar is important because it helps people to understand each other.

in nest. an egg laid its bird The

Without grammar, this sentence doesn't make sense.

This book is about **sentences**.
A sentence is a group of words.
Grammar helps you put the words in
the right order so that they make sense.

The bird laid an egg in its nest.

Grammar turns the
jumbled-up words
into a sentence.

What Is a Sentence?

A **sentence** begins with a **capital letter**. It ends with a **period** or another type of **punctuation mark**.

The dog is chasing a ball.

This sentence starts with a capital "T" and ends with a period.

A sentence must also have a **verb** (a doing word) and it must make sense on its own. Look at the examples below.

I got a.

This is not a sentence. It doesn't make sense on its own.

I got a new bike.

This is a sentence. It makes sense on its own.

Make a Sentence

On these two pages, there are some groups of words that are jumbled up. Can you turn them into **sentences**?

animals lots are There zoo. in the of

The monkeys. zookeeper fed the

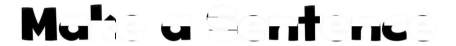

The correct answers are: There are lots of animals in the zoo. The zookeeper fed the monkeys.

Remember that a sentence starts with a **capital letter** and ends with a **punctuation mark**. It must make sense on its own. Here are two more examples for you to try.

party. I to went birthday a

ice cream. cake and ate lots I of

The correct answers are: I went to a birthday party. I ate lots of cake and ice cream.

Statements

There are different types of **sentences**. They do different jobs. A statement is a sentence that simply tells you something.

The monster was big and scary.

This sentence is a statement.

Today, it is raining.

In this statement, "it is raining" is a fact.

In writing, you use statements to tell your readers about facts. Statements always end with a **period**.

Questions

A question is a **sentence** that asks for an answer. The sentence below is an example of a question.

This is a question. The answer might be "yes" or "no."

Do you want to play soccer?

A question begins with a **capital letter**. It ends with a **question mark** instead of a **period**.

> **Why do I need a haircut?**

This is a question. It has a question mark at the end.

Exclamations

An exclamation is a **sentence** that says something strongly or with feeling. It can also show surprise.

This is an exclamation. It shows that the person writing feels strongly about chocolate.

I hate chocolate!

There is a dinosaur in the park!

This is an exclamation. It has an exclamation point at the end.

An exclamation begins with a **capital letter**. It ends with an **exclamation point** instead of a **period**.

Commands

A command is when you tell someone to do something. You give someone an order.

This is a command. You are giving an order.

Clean your teeth properly.

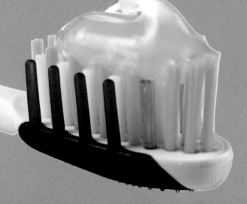

A command usually starts with a **verb**. You sometimes put an **exclamation point** at the end.

Don't eat all the cookies!

This is a command.
It has an exclamation
point at the end.

Simple Sentences

A simple **sentence** has two parts. The first part is the subject. This is the person or thing that the sentence is about.

Holly built a sandcastle.

"Holly" is the subject. The sentence is about her.

The second part of a sentence is what is written or said about the subject. It always has a **verb** in it.

The fish swim in the sea.

The second part of this sentence is "swim in the sea." "Swim" is the verb.

Adding Other Words

You can make your **sentences** more interesting by adding some **adjectives**. Adjectives are words that describe **nouns** (naming words).

"Enormous" is an adjective. It describes "sandcastle," which is a noun.

Holly built an enormous sandcastle.

The fish swim **slowly** in the sea.

"Slowly" is an adverb. It describes "swims," which is a verb.

You could also try adding **adverbs** to your sentences. Adverbs are words that describe **verbs** (doing words).

Joining Sentences

Lots of short **sentences** can be difficult to read. Try joining sentences together. This will help your writing or speech to flow better.

> I like playing tennis. My sister likes playing soccer.

Here are two short sentences. They do not flow very well.

You use **conjunctions** to join sentences together. A conjunction is a joining word, such as "and," "but," "when," or "because."

"But" is a conjunction. It joins the two sentences together.

I like playing tennis, **but** my sister likes playing soccer.

Phrases

You can make your **sentences** longer by adding **phrases**. A phrase is a group of words. It does not have a **verb** and is not a sentence.

"Across the field" is a phrase.

The horse ran across the field.

Phrases also help to make sentences sound more interesting. You can use them instead of simple **nouns**.

The big, green crocodile **had sharp teeth.**

You add "big" and "green" to "crocodile" to make a phrase.

Clauses

You can also add **clauses** to your **sentences**. A clause is a group of words that *does* have a **verb**.

> **I ate six cakes** because I was hungry.

"Because I was hungry" is a clause and "was" is the verb used.

The sentence below is made up of two clauses. Each clause has a verb. Each clause works on its own as a simple sentence.

Both of these clauses work on their own.
Joe walked to school.
Sophie rode her bike.

Joe walked to school, but Sophie rode her bike.

Paragraphs

A **paragraph** is a group of **sentences**. The sentences are all about the same thing. Putting your sentences into paragraphs makes your writing easier to read.

Once there was a fierce dragon. It lived in a dark cave under the ground. It guarded a big treasure chest.

This paragraph has three sentences.

Once there was a fierce dragon. It lived in a dark cave under the ground. It guarded a big treasure chest.

The dragon liked breathing fire so it didn't have many friends. Sometimes, it felt very lonely.

The new paragraph starts a little way in from the edge.

In a new paragraph, start the first line a little way in from the edge of the page. This makes it easier to see where the new paragraph begins.

U_i_g Senten_e_

How many **sentences** can you use to describe what is happening here?

Possible answers

The cow is eating leaves. The brown cow is eating dandelion leaves. The cow ate the leaves while the other cows watched. The cow filled its mouth with leaves, under a cloudy sky. Three cows looked at the camera, while the photographer took their picture.

Glossary

adjective describing word that tells you more about a noun

adverb describing word that tells you more about a verb

capital letter upper-case letter, such as A, B, C, D, E

clause group of words that does have a verb

conjunction word that joins sentences together

exclamation point mark at the end of a sentence to show a strong feeling

grammar a set of rules that helps you to speak or write clearly

noun a naming word

question mark mark at the end of a sentence to show a question

paragraph group of sentences

period mark that shows the end of a sentence

phrase group of words that does not have a verb

punctuation mark mark used in writing to make the meaning clear

sentence group of words that make sense on their own

verb a doing or action word

Find Out More

Books

Cleary, Brian P. *Slide and Slurp, Scratch and Burp: More About Verbs.* Minneapolis, MN: Lerner, 2010.

Shaskan, Trisha Sue Speed. If You Were a Capital Letter. Mankato, MN: Picture Window Books, 2007.

Website

www.funbrain.com/grammar/
This fun Website asks readers to spot the parts of speech in different sentences.

Index